Blockchain Made Simple
- a Non-Technical Explanation

Smart contracts - Supply chain management - Relief efforts - Medical research - Epidemiology - and, yes, least important, Bitcoin.

From IBM to the UN, blockchain is already impacting how large organizations work.`

Copyright © 2018 Groundhog Press Inc.

No part of this document may be reproduced or transmitted in any form or by any means, electronic, mechanical, photocopying, recording, or otherwise, without prior written permission of Groundhog Press Inc. or the author.

Introduction: Why blockchain? 4
Chapter 1 What is blockchain? 9
Chapter 2 Distributed Ledgers 13
Chapter 3 Libraries, Blockchain, and the Information Economy 15
Chapter 4 Blockchain in Medicine 18
Chapter 5 Business & Government Implications 27
Chapter 6 Financial Sector Applications 31
Chapter 7 Reaching Consensus via Proof of Work and Proof of Stake 33
Chapter 8 Directed Acyclic Graphs 36
Chapter 9 Hashcash - Fighting Spam - Guaranteeing Blockchain 39
Chapter 10 Cryptocurrencies (Bitcoin) 41
Chapter 11 Mining - Creating Your Own Money 51
Appendix I Resources 55

Introduction: Why blockchain?

Why should you learn about blockchain?

After all, you have zero interest in cryptocurrencies, the semi-mythical money backed by nothing but complex encryption, not gold, not silver, not even a government or a bank.

But blockchain has almost nothing to do with Bitcoins.

Bitcoin is to blockchain as spam is to email.

That is, you can't have spam without email - so too you can't have Bitcoins without blockchain. But there is much to be celebrated with email.

Besides cryptocurrencies, we already see blockchain being applied to digital contracts, financial and public records, and property ownership.

Upcoming advances will see applications in medicine, science, education, supply chain management, and even intellectual property (books and music).

Blockchain impact on business will be enormous as the technology matures. To cite just one disruptive example, smart contracts could dramatically reduce the need for business lawyers.

Consider a self-actualizing or "smart" contract - that is, a contract to perhaps deliver 100 widgets of a certain color in exchange for $100 on delivery. In a contract managed through blockchain you don't need a lawyer to manage the contract or a centralized clearinghouse to guarantee the transaction; you can get paid automatically as soon as the buyer accepts delivery.

Blockchain technology is poised to disrupt the entire business legal structure by eliminating a large portion of it.

The BLOCK in blockchain is a chunk of information. Each individual block containing additions or corrections to that original block contains information about every proceeding block and is hence a chain of blocks or a blockchain.

>Today the UN is using blockchain technology to manage humanitarian crisis through eleven UN agencies.
>Medical researchers say blockchain could greatly improve many aspects of medical practice and especially health administration tasks, including information sharing in clinical trials, electronic health records, drug management, education, and insurance. Upwards of $100 million is going to be spent on medical applications of blockchain technology in 2019 alone.
>In fifteen years, when the government catches up with technology, your medical records from every doctor, lab, hospital, and pharmacy will be available to your doctor in one secure place.
>Blockchain technology is already being used to keep track of perhaps a billion dollars worth of diamonds from the raw mined rock through sale, cutting, resale, incorporation in jewelry, and finally sale of the jewelry.
>The music industry is about to be turned on its head when artists can directly bill downloaders.
>IBM is investing in blockchain in a big way, beginning with supply chain management, and they have a pretty

good track record in technology - remember, the first PC was the IBM PC.

>Microsoft is developing a positive ID system for 1.1 billion people to use.

>Banks, including international powerhouses such as JP Morgan/Chase, are already developing blockchain applications.

The January-February 2017 issue of The Harvard Business Review looked at the promise of blockchain technology, emphasizing that it may take decades to completely alter business processes but reminds readers that applications of TCP/IP (Transmission Control Protocol/ Internet Protocol - i.e., the Internet) were proposed in 1972 but popular email services didn't begin to be seen until 1996 - since then the Internet has completely transformed the world.

https://enterprisersproject.com/sites/default/files/the_truth_about_blockchain.pdf

By this point it should be clear that blockchain will impact every aspect of business; therefore, you NEED to understand what blockchain is as this new technology is poised to rapidly become the most important new computer development over the next decade or two.

In that time frame and, given the speed of technological advances, perhaps even sooner, blockchain will trigger as significant a change in how business operates as email, spreadsheets, or word processing software did.

Blockchain will save time and therefore costs. That alone guarantees government and business will push to adopt blockchain processes as soon as possible.

Blockchain will even provide new ways to track food from farm to table, greatly improving food safety.

Why this booklet?

Unlike far too many books and articles about blockchain technology, this won't tax your patience or strain your brain by concentrating on complex mathematical formulas or focusing on what is the first but actually one of the least important applications of blockchain - Bitcoin.

Read on and near the end (where they belong) I will explain what Bitcoin and other cryptocurrencies (money based on cryptography or codes) are but remember that they are far less important than the technology behind them and I include cryptocurrencies in a later chapter only as one concrete but minor example of blockchain technology.

However, don't be concerned - although the details are esoteric involving complex mathematics, the basic facts about blockchain really are quite simple.

That may sound very strange since most of what you have read or heard about blockchain probably makes it seem extremely complex and you probably don't see what cryptography has to do with your business or even your personal money.

But you actually use financial encryption technology every day - your credit cards, ATM transactions, and even paper checks all work today BECAUSE of cryptography.

By saying blockchain is quite simple, I mean that just as with email, or word processing, or 802.11 (the WiFi standard), most people don't want or even need to understand the actual technical details or programming used in order to make full use of the technology.

Consider this; you probably have no idea how your cell phone works, whether your carrier is CDMA or GSM, or that optical disks from the original CD-ROM players to the latest Blu-ray movies are based on the compact OS-9 Unix operating system first made popular in the old Radio Shack pre-PC Color Computer.

But, even knowing nothing about the underlying technology, you can still use that cell phone to call your sister or BFF and use your Blu-ray player to watch the latest movie.

Similarly, although blockchain can't exist without very sophisticated encryption technology and will become even more important with the development of useful quantum encryption, all you really need to know about encryption technology is that it works.

If you need a quick proof that you don't need to understand the details about how blockchain works to make use of it, skip to the Business Implications chapter to learn about a downloadable app that lets you create your own smart contract or even a new cryptocurrency.

Chapter 1 What is blockchain?

Fundamentally, blockchain technologies are a distributed ledger scheme - that means precisely what the words indicate, a ledger, record, or block of information, documents, or events that is stored in a distributed fashion.

In other words, blockchain is a record or database consisting of blocks of data that is kept in multiple places, with copies of the file folder, but with exact provably identical copies of the folder itself spread across multiple locations, all of which hold the complete record, are synchronized, contain a complete history of the elements of each block, and are therefore identical.

The records can only be modified by someone with permission, that is, who has the encryption key necessary to access the data.

A record kept in multiple locations is MORE secure than one kept in only one place.

Not only that, but when any alteration is made to the ledger that change is also traceable and proveable.

For example, if a Bitcoin is spent that fact is recorded in all records about that unit of value.

Blockchain technology was initially developed for the currency known as Bitcoin but can, will, and already has been applied to business activities including supply chain management, traditional financial transactions, stock brokerage, enhancing food safety, and assisting in epidemiological disease studies (Centers for Disease Control) as well as humanitarian efforts (United Nations).

The correct way of looking at blockchain is as a distributed database with records guaranteed by **consensus algorithms**. That gets a bit complex, so it is covered in another chapter of this booklet. For practical purposes you don't need to know any more about consensus algorithms than that they work and that they guarantee that all copies of a particular ledger are always kept identical.

How this is accomplished will be covered later, but only in broad terms - all the various terminology surrounding blockchain technology such as Consensus Algorithms, Distributed Ledger Technologies, Directed Acyclic Graphs, and more, will be explained in plain English.

That means they will only be described approximately, not at a computer science level, but sufficiently well that you can discuss them with any layperson or even a computer scientist as long as you stick to non-mathematical language and avoid the details of algorithms.

This may seem too simplistic an approach for a serious understanding, or even a detailed enough understanding to make business plans concerning blockchain technology, but I ask you whether you have any trouble creating contracts, memoranda of understanding, and other critical business documents on your computer even though you couldn't program a new word processor from scratch in, say, C or C+. I actually could (I wrote basic versions of such programs decades ago). But even with an extensive background in computer technology I can't create a new blockchain algorithm, at least not without some serious study and skull sweat.

These days, in fact, with cloud computing platforms such as Google Drive, you don't even need to have a word processor, database, or spreadsheet installed on your computer to be able to use them.

Even this document is being created in the cloud via Google Drive because it is more efficient. It simultaneously produces both a local and remote backup copy of work in progress, and includes the ability to share and collaborate on the content of the document with others around the globe.

Working in the cloud doesn't require me to install updates; I can access and work on the text from any device with a browser, and it doesn't even cost anything.

Think about how big a change just moving software from your PC to the cloud has made when you consider the uses of blockchain technology. Even though I do actually understand how cloud computing works, even the technical details, there is absolutely no need for you to have that knowledge to make full use of cloud computing.

At this stage of the computer revolution many new businesses are developed using programs that people know how to use but not how to create - software technology has now moved far beyond the need to understand what an optimizing compiler is or does and people can and do start new businesses using computer technology without a clue as to the difference between an interpreted and a compiled computer language.

If you are really interested, a compiled language turns your program into machine language (just zeros and ones - the same as the first program I wrote in 1963) that the computer's brain (CPU) can execute directly. An interpreted language itself has to reside on the computer and creates machine usable instructions one line at a time just when it is being run - your Windows PC still has the old PC programming commands and language inside - that is what you deal with when you open the command prompt.

You can still download a free version of BASIC for Windows computers or access the hundreds of command prompt tools to do advanced programming on your PC. In Windows 95/98 the tools were BASIC; in later versions of Windows there are up to 280 special commands that only work at the command prompt window - some are part of the old BASIC language and others are new. https://www.lifewire.com/list-of-command-prompt-commands-4092302)

(Even BASIC is misunderstood - there is nothing basic about BASIC. which is actually an acronym for Beginners All purpose Symbolic Instruction Code - not so "basic" after all. https://en.wikipedia.org/wiki/BASIC

But, of course, the point I am trying to reinforce is that you probably didn't know any of that yet you use your computer daily for dozens of tasks.

The same will hold true for blockchain technology. Once it is integrated into a business application you will probably never even know it is there.

But there is money to be saved and even made by those who understand enough about the new technology to apply it to business.

Chapter 2 Distributed Ledgers

A ledger in the sense of blockchain transactions is just what you think of as a ledger in business accounting - a record or collection of records in other words **a file, a.k.a. a "block"** of information.

Distributed also means just what you think it means in plain English - the ledger is not stored in just one place but as with any process involving records there are backups or copies.

That's common business practice, keeping backups, but when they are on paper or stored on optical disks in some vault there is no way to keep them updated to the millisecond.

So, how are the people who rely on the distributed record to know that the record hasn't been altered either intentionally or accidentally?

Simple. (Remember, this is the simplified explanation, not including the computer science details.)

Each record is encrypted, can only be changed by a person with the encryption code, and every time any change is made, such as spending a Bitcoin or adding an entry to the record, or moving a commodity one further step along the supply chain, that change is a new block that is also encrypted and distributed to every location or "node" where a copy of the record is kept.

Another thing to remember is that there isn't actually any backup in the usual sense. No particular record at some node is the base or original record. They are all equal.

So, how are these records kept current and how do you know if one copy hasn't been updated correctly?

That's where the magic of blockchain technology comes into play.

You can **think of blockchain as being a chain of blocks** stretching back in time to the original creation of the record and each containing record of previous changes.

Blockchain - the creators used their imagination in creating the technology, not the name.

Each individual block of information (no matter what kind of information is involved and that is important) can be viewed as pulling along a trail of earlier states of the block, each step cryptographically locked and guaranteed to be unalterable.

For those who really thirst for technical details, the currently most used cryptographic algorithm for Bitcoins is SHA-256 cryptographic hash (https://en.wikipedia.org/wiki/SHA-256) a 256 bit (32 byte) relatively secure description of the previous block in the chain is stored in the subsequent block.

There is no possible reason why, if you are merely implementing a blockchain system, you need to know any more details about SHA-256 than that it is nearly unique, not highly secure, but good enough because of the complexity of the rest of the system.

Chapter 3 Libraries, Blockchain, and the Information Economy

If you don't know that the economies of the advanced countries from India to the U.S. are already based on the creation and exchange of knowledge or information, then you aren't paying attention. That is at the core of the discontent among a large segment of the labor class - manufacturing is a dying industry - knowledge workers are in great demand.

In fact there are constantly job openings for several million knowledge workers in the U.S. Many of these jobs only require a year or two of technical training but the U.S. school system has mostly failed to prepare and equip the vast majority of people to be able to continue learning. Math and science are NOT required to graduate high schools so an economy based on science or math literate workers is not open to most people.

Those religious schools that deny science do an even worse job than the average public school that simply ignores math beyond arithmetic and science beyond eighth grade Earth Science.

So, is it any wonder that blockchain, a new way of managing information, is going to have a great impact on how information is managed?

In the future, libraries will have a much greater impact on communities than they do today where they mostly serve as a storage and lending service for books and electronic information in the form of movies, lectures, and more.

Those are important functions that libraries have pursued for centuries but, as blockchain technology matures, advanced libraries will build greater metadata centers, provide a way to protect digital first sale rights, and help facilitate cooperation between various organizations.

Inter-Planetary File System

The strikingly named IPFS is simply a peer-to-peer library protocol for a new kind of Internet that bypasses the controls of Internet service providers (ISPs) just as cryptocurrencies bypass governments and banks.

Many people already use Internet services at public libraries and the IPFS protocol will use blockchain technology to provide a new kind of Internet access with major implications for vastly increased security and privacy.

Using this system, libraries and universities can provide the validation of credentials of any website, yours or one you are trying to access, eliminating many scams and foreign attempts to manipulate elections by presenting false information and propaganda masquerading as legitimate news.

Keeping It Real (local)

Libraries looking to become more involved in and of greater service to their local community may want to host a community-based lending system and database of local resources such as the contents of small local museums, and any community service groups that provide assistance to the needy or are lending items to locals.

In this case a library could use blockchain systems to keep track of the original owner, who has borrowed it in the past, and who has it now.

The commodities being recorded might be a vehicle, specialized tools, even a record of people who have special expertise.

Chapter 4 Blockchain in Medicine

One of the most important applications of blockchain technology for the average person is the way it can and almost certainly will alter the way medical records are stored and can be shared with hospitals and new doctors in an emergency.

A January 2017 Harris Poll found that in the U.S. only nine percent of consumers believe that big pharma puts the needs and welfare of patients first. It also asked about medical insurance firms and there the news was very slightly better, with 16 percent of healthcare insurers putting patients before profits.

Unfortunately doctors and nurses only rate about twice as well, with about 34 percent of patients believing they put patients before profits.

With that low level of trust, rivaling the ratings often found for Congress and the press, a new technology that promises a better way to manage medical information can only benefit everyone involved, especially doctors and patients.

Medicine will be impacted by blockchain technology in two or three main areas depending on how you classify them - insurance and payments, patient-centered healthcare, and clinical research. Epidemiology will also be changed by the application of this technology but that is probably more related to the way libraries and information technology is managed.

The most important part of diagnosing an illness is usually to get a complete patient history.

Anyone who has had several doctors, either due to different medical conditions or because they (as virtually every American has) have moved around over the years, and especially the elderly who often need the most care and have the longest medical history, need to make their medical history available to new doctors.

This is currently incredibly difficult. Even with the changes in laws that make it mandatory to let patients access their records, it still is nearly impossible to get an electronic copy of many of your records even if they have already been digitized.

My local hospital has a patient portal that maintains a record of medications (often outdated and very difficult to edit) and laboratory results, but neither includes any information about older X-rays, MRIs, surgeries, diagnoses, or even a list of previous doctors.

HIPAA was a great advance in protecting patient medical records but it also made doctors and hospitals very gun-shy about sharing patient information even with the patient, and especially with other doctors or hospitals.

Blockchain applications for electronic records, insurance, medication history will make it easier for doctors to correctly diagnose and treat patients by making the records available yet impossible to alter.

Tracking drugs from the manufacturer to pharmacy to end users will be much easier and more accurate, using blockchain supply chain management.

Sharing information on biomedical research, epidemiology, and even medical education will all be fundamentally changed for the good in the next decade by new blockchain applications that are barely even envisioned by the most advanced companies today.

Hundreds of millions of U.S. dollars are expected to be invested in new medically related technologies in the next few years.

Although there are still problems involving scalability (Bitcoin is greatly limited by the amount of computing power needed to manage the currency), security, and especially user adoption by healthcare organizations and individual doctors are just some of the development challenges still faced by adoption of blockchain tools, but the potential savings and increase in efficiency are compelling.

Data Integrity

As patients, laboratory results, and other data increase, it becomes more difficult to process and store the massive amount of data.

Data being managed include patient health information, electronic health records, Internet linked monitoring systems, insurance claims, and more.

Blockchain will help guarantee that such recorded data will be encrypted and impossible to alter or delete.

If the ledgers of data blocks are locked by blockchain technology, it will be easy for anyone who has legitimately authorized access can see the data and both verify their accuracy and completeness without a need to rely on any third party to guarantee that integrity. That will reduce the expense involved in regulatory compliance and medical audits.

HIPAA legal requirements for electronic record security can be burdensome - blockchain will reduce both cost and time to protect medical records because the technology is much more secure than simple encryption.

Even if hackers were able to break into a record database, they wouldn't be able to make any changes.

Although the encryption used for blockchain is relatively weak and therefore easy to implement, you can think of blockchain as multiple layers of that encryption.

Hyperledger is an umbrella project begun in 2015 by the Linux Foundation, which was already working to apply blockchain to medical records.

Lack of knowledge about what blockchain is and how it works is already delaying implementation in the medical arena.

Disintermediation is a term you will often see in discussions of blockchain technology but the underlying concept is easy to understand; essentially, disintermediation just means reducing the number of people or companies between the producer and the consumer - in this case, between doctors and patients.

Reducing the number of steps between supplier and consumer always reduces costs; whether they are passed along or retained as increased profits is another question.

Blockchain helps with disintermediation, data integrity, and provenance (origin) for drugs, medical, and insurance records; those are seen as the most important advantages of applying the new technology to medical practice.

Caregivers who already understand the basics of blockchain say they are anxious to apply it to their particular organization.

There are three main ways already being envisioned as perfect opportunities to utilize blockchain in a medical environment.

> Drug traceability;
>Data security in clinical trials;
And
>Patient Data Management.

One of the big problems today in the distribution end of pharmacology is the threat posed by counterfeit drugs being slipped into the supply chain. Not only will a counterfeit drug not provide the therapeutic benefit expected, it could be actively harmful. The Health Research Funding Organization reports that between 10 and 30 percent of all the drugs in Third World countries are fake. This costs drug companies hundreds of billions every year and harm millions of patients.

Applying blockchain to pharmaceuticals means that every pill can be tracked from the manufacturer of the basic chemicals shipped to the pharmaceutical company to when it is dispensed at a pharmacy. Since records in blockchain can't be altered and each carries a timestamp, it is easy to identify counterfeit drugs and makes it much easier for law enforcement to pin down the time when the drugs entered the supply chain and hence trace their origin.

Clinical trials are critical to finding effective new treatments for diseases and are the only way many treatments and especially drugs can be approved by the FDA.

But precisely because they are so important to both the drug companies that produce the drugs or treatment and the researchers who get big grants to run the clinical trials, there are always the potential and incentive to commit fraud by altering the trial records and the data collected.

This fraud potential leads to the need to apply blockchain technology in an effort to provide impenetrable security for the data collected in clinical trials.

Whether data are manipulated to make a drug more effective than it really is, or to conceal dangerous side effects, the researchers who make a living conducting clinical trials have a strong incentive to keep drug companies happy with their work.

A lot of data are collected during a clinical trial (I've been involved in one) and it is quite easy to misplace a report or modify a few numbers when everything is being done on paper or on a local computer owned and managed by the people running the trial.

Blockchain provides a way to prove the origin and accuracy of data and, by maintaining a distributed set of copies of the records adds to the security of the entire process. It also helps insulate the testers from pressure applied by any unscrupulous individuals in big pharma.

If blockchain is applied to a clinical trial, it makes it much, much more difficult to manipulate the data and therefore a lot easier for the researchers to resist any attempt to manipulate the results.

Studies have proven that this application of blockchain technology does provide an easy way to provably secure the data.

Patient records are now given very strong protection by the Health Insurance Portability and Accountability Act or HIPAA, which requires that all patient data be kept secure.

But the problem with HIPAA is that, because of the strict privacy requirements, it is virtually impossible even for the patient to obtain a copy of his or her own medical record.

Patients seldom need to see their own records of course, but they will commonly want or need to share their records with pharmacies or other doctors and while HIPAA added privacy protection it has made it virtually impossible for an emergency room 1,000 miles away to pick up the phone and request medical information about an incoming accident victim.

Blockchain security can be designed in such a way that legitimate medical needs can be easily verified - for example, an actual record request from a real ER doctor could be automatically approved.

Blockchain creates a new secure and unique encryption hash for every block of patient data.

One thing blockchain can do is make it easy to obtain the medical data for patients with a certain disease yet completely secure and hide the patient's identity, which is just as good as keeping the records themselves secret as far as HIPAA is concerned.

After all, what does it matter if a lot of medical information from blood pressure to cholesterol levels is seen in a record if there is no way to tell to which of a hundred million people the record applies?

That sort of information about patient conditions, tests, treatments, and outcome already exists and would be an incredible resource for medical researchers.

Hiding patient identity using blockchain tools protects privacy.

However, if you are the person whose records are being accessed by a new doctor you can easily prove that they are your records.

Although medical organizations are slow to implement and adopt blockchain technology there are some notable examples.

Guardtime is a system that secures patient data.

Bem Health looks to advance collaboration among various healthcare organizations using blockchain.

Cyph seems to be focused mainly on securing the identity of the person associated with a set of data.

And there are other new applications being planned and put forward almost daily.

So, if you are healthy, why should you be concerned with all this?

Simple enough; if there is an easy way to access masses of medical records without any bureaucratic dance and without any concern about disclosing the medical records tied to a particular individual, government organizations such as the CDC (Centers for Disease Control and Prevention) can track the health of an entire population with data mining techniques as long as the records' personal identities are locked away by blockchain.

This means the CDC can track new infections and the FDA can monitor the effectiveness of drug treatment protocols.

On the insurance side, it is estimated that there is about $50 billion of insurance fraud just in the U.S. and access to the metadata identity protected yet readily available through blockchain can greatly reduce this burden - remember, insurance companies have to make money and consumers end up paying for fraud, just like emergency room visits by the uninsured are eventually paid for by everyone else.

On a personal level, just consider how much better care you can recieve in an emergency if first responders can access your medical and especially pharmaceutical history combined with the many new wearable technology tools that monitors your health daily.

Chapter 5 Business & Government Implications

Just as business was the first place we saw major widespread applications of personal computers (remember the IBM in IBM PC was originally International Business Machines), it is no surprise that businesses were the first to see the benefits and begin to adopt blockchain based systems.

Two business applications immediately present themselves.

The first is supply chain management.

The second is creating and using smart contracts that eliminate many steps and people (lawyers and law firms) normally required to implement even simple contracts.

It should be obvious that blockchain can be applied to management of the supply chain.

The origin and quality of supplies can be recorded and tracked through every step of the supply chain.

Supply chain management is basically tracking products, whether material goods or services.
The supply chain begins with the creation, movement, and storage of raw materials such as chemicals.

It continues by tracking the movement through manufacturing, inventory, transport of finished goods, to consumption.

Blockchain even sounds a bit like supply chain and applying the technology to supply chain management is one of the most obvious business applications.

Another obvious business application for blockchain, one that can benefit any size business from a garage-based eBay home business to a multinational, is the ability to create something often referred to as a smart contract.

A smart contract is one that holds the funding or other fulfillment for a transaction and can directly execute itself by disbursing the money or other payment when a certain transaction goal is met. Or perhaps it will execute automatically on a specific date.

But the critical point about a smart contract is that it exists and can be a complete transaction without any recourse to the legal system, either a law firm or a clearinghouse.

In other words, a smart contract increases disintermediation - it reduces the number of people and processes required to complete a contractual obligation and may completely remove an organization that formerly managed contract compliance, such as a law firm.

Eliminating the steps and people involved in a contract obviously saves time and money, both dear to the hearts of any MBA.

Ethereum

In fact, this is such a powerful concept that you can produce a smart contract today through the Ethereum.org website and, by the time you read this, probably other sites.

Data Sharing

Another application for blockchain technology in the average business will be to make it easier to share data.

In most IT architectures, each application is configured to reside and run on a different server.

This makes sharing data either more difficult if proper security steps are implemented, or, if not, it leaves the data more vulnerable to compromise.

Startups such as Ethereum (ethereum.org) create wallets for blockchain smart contracts that are used to keep records of debts or instructions to execute certain steps at a specific time or at a set time.

Everledger (everledger.io) is a blockchain system for keeping track of individual valuable assets. Everledger is already being used to keep track of the IDs of a million individual diamonds, which can protect against theft and also ensure the provenance of a gem to prove it isn't a "blood" or conflict diamond.

Smart contracts created by either company can include such parameters as weather conditions (commodity value), stock prices, or virtually any other quantifiable data.

Verisart (verisart.com) is a startup trying to develop a blockchain database of art objects that can be used to prove the authenticity and origin of paintings or sculptures.

Block Verify (blockverify) is doing the same thing for a variety of very high value items, tracking sales and helping identify stolen goods. The startup says the same tools can be applied to tracking counterfeit drugs.

But not all blockchain solutions involve start-ups.

Coco Framework (https://azure.microsoft.com/en-us/blog/announcing-microsoft-s-coco-framework-for-enterprise-blockchain-networks/) is a Microsoft project to manage supply chain and business relationships.

IBM has a Hyperledger Fabric codebase application called IBM blockchain (https://www.ibm.com/blockchain/).

Sony has as yet (as of this writing) an unnamed project using blockchain as a platform to store information about students including identity and academic records.

Southern New Hampshire University is testing a program that will provide alumni with a way to apply blockchain-implemented digital credentials verifying their educational background.

DECODE is the European Union government project that can maintain a record of citizen preferences about what personal data they will and won't permit to be shared.

Other obvious government applications include tracking any kind of record from birth certificates to driver's licenses, deeds, and more.

All of these applications could impose massive computing loads on existing systems and probably can't be fully implemented until computer technology progresses another generation or two.

Chapter 6 Financial Sector Applications

The most important thing to remember about blockchain technology is that it provides a secure, encrypted decentralized register recording every transaction from the initial formation of the data block to the current state.
You may be thinking that sounds like exactly what a bank does. It is.
Every computer involved in the system stores another copy of the information block.
Before permitting a new transaction the originating system must confirm whether there is another blockchain related record, i.e. whether the requested transaction is permissible - are the funds available?
Using blockchain brokerages can more easily track transactions while government agencies can watch for insider trading patterns (fraud that hurts every other investor).
It is easy to think of such crimes and frauds as being none of your business, but any unscrupulous or illegal siphoning of monies out of any business just means that everyone else has to pay a bit more - sometimes a lot more.
That's probably all I need to say about financial applications of blockchain until a later chapter which looks at cryptocurrencies such as Bitcoin.
Although I said at the outset that blockchain wasn't really about Bitcoin, that very first application of the technology does show how the technology works. You don't have to want to hide your money in cyberspace or

avoid government monetary systems to see the advantages of blockchain as shown by the origin of blockchain.

Chapter 7 Reaching Consensus via Proof of Work and Proof of Stake

This chapter begins a look at the underlying technology that makes blockchain work.

You don't really need even this non-technical explanation to implement a blockchain application but if you want to present the concept at a board meeting you should probably learn some of the basic terminology if not the technical details.

Consensus, or rather a consensus algorithm, is at the core of blockchain technology and there are two basic ways of generating consensus, Proof of Work or PoW and Proof of Stake or PoS.

PoW is currently the main current route to blockchain consensus as exemplified by Bitcoin mining. PoW today involves the computer time required to solve moderately complex cryptographic or other computationally difficult problems.

The level of work required for PoW consensus is easy to adjust to match the importance of the records. Simply make the cryptographic problem more or less difficult.

This should be familiar to some readers as being related to the use of cryptography and factoring large numbers.

For Bitcoin the PoW computation chain is known as mining; hence, you will hear about Bitcoin mining. For the first Bitcoin this was easy but each new Bitcoin becomes more difficult to create because the amount of computation required increases.

Today creating a new Bitcoin is very expensive in computer power.

There are about 17 million Bitcoins in existence but there is also a finite limit on how many can ever be created - that limit is 21 million individual Bitcoins.

For the details go to the Cryptocurrency and Bitcoin chapter where I will explain how to create your own Bitcoins - be warned it was easy at first but now requires a special computer chip and a big electric bill to create the next Bitcoin.

Once again, to make use of blockchain or plan to implement it in your business, you don't need to know the details to be aware that it is very computationally difficult, i.e. time-consuming, to work with large prime numbers.

PoW or Proof of Work is a simple concept first developed to combat spam (the junk email, not the canned meat). The idea behind spam is simple since it costs nothing to send an email if you send 10 million you will hit a score or more gullible or careless people.

Proof of Work simply adds a requirement that any email accepted by the various big email systems such as Google's Gmail must contain a header that includes not only the address of the target recipient, but also solves a math problem.

By adjusting the difficulty of the problem you can make the sender prove he or she did the work and although it is a miniscule amount of computational power for a friend's one email, it becomes too expensive for spammers to send millions of junk emails.

By adding PoW to the blockchain it becomes ever more expensive to create new Bitcoins and also blocks casual attacks against any blockchain.

PoS is less expensive, that is, easier and faster to accomplish and may be the best consensus process for many applications.

However, PoS is actually a rather vague concept and the fact that it is computationally easy means that there is no built in penalty for cheating. Various proposals exist for getting around this and other PoS faults but while some cryptocurrencies using PoS do exist, e.g. Peercoin and Ethereum, there is no widely adopted consensus on how to apply the PoS consensus algorithm concept.

Peercoin (https://en.wikipedia.org/wiki/Peercoin) first applied PoS using cryptographic private keys.

Ethereum's Slasher protocol included a cost on forgers but that didn't work.

There is a concept known as PoB or Proof of Burn, which is combined with PoS. Not being practical I see no reason to burden you with any details of that failed protocol.

Several combinations of these systems have been suggested; most involve a different balance combining PoS and PoS.

Because the difficult and easy protocols can be balanced in various applications this may prove to be a practical way of implementing blockchain.

The hybrid system PoW would provide the difficulty of mining blocks while PoS, which by itself has no penalty, would provide a secondary method of authenticating the validity of the data - that makes it harder to cheat but easier to verify a legitimate transaction or record.

Proof of Stake (https://en.wikipedia.org/wiki/Proof-of-stake)

Chapter 8 Directed Acyclic Graphs

Hold onto your hats; this is where it starts to get complicated, in other words real computer science territory, but I'll try to keep things understandable by people who didn't major in math or computer science at university (I only majored in math since there was no computer science major back then).

Put as simply as possible, Directed Acyclic Graphics (DAGs) are just a way of modeling the way information is organized.

That's not entirely accurate but is close enough for our purposes.

DAG is part of a branch of mathematics (and computer science) that studies graphs. Unsurprisingly this is known as Graph Theory.

https://en.wikipedia.org/wiki/Graph_theory

If you want to learn more about Graph Theory you should probably look at this introduction to Graph Theory. A Gentle Introduction To Graph Theory – basecs – Medium

https://medium.com/basecs/a-gentle-introduction-to-graph-theory-77969829ead8

Graph Theory lets you present a problem in a simple visual form that can be solved perhaps at a glance even though the mathematics underlying a rigorous proof is too complicated to perform.

You may be familiar with a common IQ test problem where you are asked to find a path where someone can proceed across a series of bridges crossing every one only once.

This was first solved by a mathematician named Euler, using graphs - it was simply too difficult to solve by calculation before computers.

In computer science graphs are often used to represent many different things such as the flow of computations, communication networks, and more.

This may be because even in the early days we produced a visual flowchart showing how a computer program worked even before any of the actual programming took place.

A flowchart shows the logic involved and makes it relatively easy to see any errors.

The application to blockchain is simple in concept. Graphical analysis of a blockchain process is a basic way of working out how a particular blockchain application might work.

Again, that is a very simplistic description, but probably sufficient for most readers.

The technical term for this analysis is graph mining.

An example of how graph theory can be applied to blockchain is simple; although I have already stated that Bitcoin is only a tiny part of the story of blockchain, it turns out that all applications of blockchain technology have similar graphs, including Bitcoin.

You probably don't need to know any more about DAG than that, perhaps not even that much, but DAG is a term you will run into when looking at blockchain applications so it is important to know how it is involved.

For those who want or need to understand just how graph analysis is applied to blockchain networks read on.

Content graphs ere either transaction, address, or entity graphs.

Transaction graphs are acyclic where an edge is used to symbolize a transferred asset or transaction (such as purchased or spent Bitcoin).

An address graph is used once to indicate the place an asset is sent. These are a bad idea because they weaken the encryption.

The entity graph is involved in tracking other addresses owned by the same person or company. Addresses may be published on the Internet.

Beyond this the details of what these graphs are and how used gets into much more detail than appropriate for this booklet.

For more information about this topic see the Wikipedia link, which goes into much more detail.

Throughout this booklet I have been including these Wikipedia links because they will be updated with authoritative information as it becomes available. Although I may make some of the contributions, even those will be the equivalent of peer reviewed that has made Wikipedia the equal of any print encyclopedia and, in fact, the various Wikis often surpass print encyclopedias for accuracy. Directed Acyclic Graphs
https://en.wikipedia.org/wiki/Directed_acyclic_graph

Chapter 9 Hashcash - Fighting Spam - Guaranteeing Blockchain

Hashcash is another term you are likely to encounter in discussions of blockchain and only for that reason it is included here. Hashcash is a way to link identity with the originator of a message and was initially proposed as a way to reduce spam, which was rearing its ugly head as far back as the mid-90s.

This also provided a possible way to combat denial of service attacks.

Everyone knows what spam is but you may not understand how serious DoS and especially DDoS (Distributed DoS) attacks were in the early days when computers were much slower than now and the Internet was much more primitive.

A DoS attack basically overwhelms a server hosting a website with more requests for contact than the server can handle.

A Distributed DoS merely indicates that there are a great many sources of the attack as opposed to just a few conspirators with their bank of computers.

A recent example of what I would term a "benign" DDoS event was when in July 2018 Amazon launched a massive sales event for Prime members as a business income way of balancing the Black Friday Christmas event every year.

The deals were significant and so many Prime members tried to shop that even Amazon's massive IT infrastructure crashed, or at least it was so overwhelmed that people couldn't get in.

That is the essence of a denial of service event that can be used as a malignant attack on some institution - often a bank or other financial institution.

Hashcash is an example of the use of PoW (Proof of Work) systems described above which require the sender of an email to perform some minor calculation that is no problem for individuals or even a group mailing to several dozen or even several hundred members, but is too expensive to make it profitable to send millions of spam messages in order to hook a few suckers.

As with the following section on cryptocurrencies this chapter is not necessary to the understanding of blockchain technology but it will also dramatically change the technological basis of our civilization and make encryption in general and blockchain even more important.

Chapter 10 Cryptocurrencies (Bitcoin)

As stated briefly in the introduction, Bitcoin was created as a way to have a currency independent of banks or governments, sometimes, but not always as a way to avoid the attention of authorities wishing to tax or prevent certain transactions or prevent people from moving funds out of a country.

An example of the latter is China, which limits or makes it extremely difficult to take money out of the country.

Currently you can take as much money in or out of the United States, but this is subject to a requirement to report any amount over $10,000, which has its own chilling effect even on people who have only legitimate reasons to do so.

The most critical element that all money or currency shares is that you can only spend it once. Given a coin or paper bill that is easy. I give you a quarter to buy something and can't give it to someone else because you now have it.

Checks and bank withdrawals are the same but are controlled by banks just as governments control paper currency.

The developers of Bitcoin wanted a way to ensure their new currency could only be used (spent) once by the same person but do so without any central authority such as a bank or PayPal.

They accomplished this by recording ownership and identity and owner of each individual "coin" in multiple locations.

That, in a nutshell, is what blockchain is - a way to keep track of assets or something else (such as a document) and, critically, be confident it isn't modified or ownership is or isn't changed but without reliance on any central authority such as a government mint, bank, or credit card company.

Because Bitcoin utilizes Proof of Work (described above) in ever increasing amounts which as of mid 2018 is estimated to consume energy to the value of $15M per day through "mining" operations.

Although Bitcoin is highly secure because of the chain of records, the need for solving cryptographic problems before a transaction can be completed means that it takes time to complete any transaction and that, in turn, means there is a limit to how many Bitcoin transactions can be performed - currently that limit is something close to six transactions per second, a fact that virtually guarantees that Bitcoin can never become a major monetary system. In comparison the VISA network can process tens or even hundreds of thousands of transactions each second.

Technically Bitcoin is the name given to the first creation of what is known as a "wallet" similar to a physical wallet because you can keep money in it. The details are interesting but not essential and will not be covered here.

You can skip this chapter and still understand everything you need to know about blockchain technology. I only include this chapter because Bitcoin was the first real world example of blockchain applied to the real world (by Satoshi Nakamoto - not a real person, that is the name adopted by an anonymous person or group of people).

Gold and silver have functioned as both money and currency at many times, and it is understandable that governments would object to money it can't track and control - and, most importantly, TAX!

Governments, including major democracies, also want to avoid a more widespread understanding of the difference between money and currency because people who do understand tend to notice just how bad inflation is even in the United States.

Currency (technically a fiat currency) is the representation of a value either as printed or minted symbols or electronic records. The precise value of a unit of currency is variable, in fact it is arbitrarily variable, that is, the issuer such as a government can decide it has a different value.

Before you say that's ridiculous I'll remind you that last century both FDR and Richard Nixon devalued the U.S. dollar.

Because cryptocurrencies don't depend on a central authority such as a government or bank for their value, they are not subject to that sort of manipulation (although they are subject to other manipulations).

A change in value of a fiat currency can also be the result of public belief in the value of the currency.

Money, on the other hand has an intrinsic value - an example would be back a century ago when US dollars could be exchanged for gold or silver and the coinage actually contained a large percentage of gold or silver. If you melted down a $20 gold piece in 1910 you would get about $20 worth of gold.

Silver dollars from the 1800s and early part of the 1900s contain an ounce of silver which, at that time, was priced at about $1/oz. (it is now worth about $15/oz.)

which is a measure of how the value of the dollar has dropped, NOT a measure of how much more valuable silver has become.

That's inflation, a hidden tax.

Consider that a good new car or pickup truck cost $2,000 in 1960 and $30,000 in 2018. There are many new features on today's truck, subtract them and a basic truck in 2018 still costs about ten times more than it would in 1960. That's inflation, but inflation of the dollar, not in terms of gold - it takes about the same amount of gold to buy that new truck today and when I was 12.

To discuss Bitcoin and why people might want a new kind of money we need a few simple, basic definitions because most people don't generally understand anything about money.

WHAT?? That's a foolish statement, you are probably thinking. But it really isn't. I bet 3/4 of those reading this didn't understand what a fiat currency was before I defined it above.

In fact, the actual definition of money and currency are critical to the understanding of how the world of business functions.

It is also clear that governments aren't really interested in having most people understand the difference.

Financial planners, bankers, and accountants also seldom understand the difference but anyone in a country with runaway inflation can explain it easily.

You can boil down the misunderstanding to when and why money is or is not currency and vice versa.

Gold can be money. So can paper or coins. But while physical gold and silver gives coins an intrinsic value not necessarily related to the "face" value, there is also currency, sometimes known as fiat currency.

That simply means that paper or coins have a given value because a government says it does.

When paper money in the U.S. could be exchanged for gold or silver (such as with a silver certificate) then it was both money and currency.

Money can even change into a fiat currency. For example, there was a time when you could exchange a piece of green paper for either silver or gold, the physical metals, by presenting them to the U.S. Mint.

Other governments could do so even after American citizens were forbidden to do so.

For example, you can't do that today. The paper money no longer has that guarantee printed on the paper. In fact, your paper money is not given any actual value as printed on the money itself other than being lawful for all public or private debt.

Money, by definition, is a store of value as are gold, silver, diamonds, and many other physical commodities.

Currency, on the other hand, is money in motion - from the Middle English: current, "in circulation", from Latin: currens, -entis.

Currency is a generally accepted medium of exchange.

But this is a moving target.

Silver dollars contain very nearly one ounce of silver in an alloy to make it stronger. When initially produced in the 1800s one ounce of silver was worth about $1. This value changes, mostly upward, and as I wrote above today one ounce of silver is worth about $15.

But silver has been worth as much as $50 (January 1980) and was brought back to $0.99 per ounce by Paul

Volcker, a chairman of the Federal Reserve who dumped the entire U.S. Mint's vast store of silver bullion onto the market. (That's an oversimplification but, as they say, close enough for government work.)

If the government still owned that silver it would be worth 15 times what it was when Volker had a hissy fit about the Hunt Brothers and threw it away.

Today West Point and the Denver Mint are each thought to hold about 1,500 tons of gold. The Federal Reserve in New York City has about 400 tons. The amount still in Fort Knox is unclear.

Interestingly enough although governments discourage the use of gold as a medium of exchange (even sometimes making it illegal - see F. D. Roosevelt, 1933) they insist on using gold between themselves - although Fort Knox is widely thought of as a great gold storage facility, there is actually a vast amount of physical gold in a vault beneath the streets of Manhattan and many countries have separate lockers where they store their gold. This gold is moved from locker to locker as nation's balance trade exchanges.

Everything becomes even more complicated because of inflation. Copper, for example, is worth far more than the $0.01 value given to the penny by the government. In fact, because of that the penny no longer has any significant amount of copper in it. The same goes for the nickel, which is made of 75 percent copper while the penny is made mostly of zinc.

(BTW, during WWII most pennies were made from steel. A few 1943 pennies were made from copper before the changeover. If you find one, please send it along to me. Alternatively, take it to a coin dealer who will give you $50,000 or $100,000 for it.)

Just as the U.S. dollar and most government monies today is a fiat currency, that is, only has value because the government says you must accept it as a legal way to settle a debt, so too the Bitcoin is a fiat currency - not being physical at all, it has to be.

However, a Bitcoin performs all the functions of currency; people assign a value to it and, if you own one, you can exchange it for goods or services electronically. Although this is usually done through an intermediary of some sort - a virtual bank - it can be exchanged directly or peer-to-peer.

The value of a Bitcoin is reached by a consensus between those who own or want to own Bitcoins. That probably sounds crazy, but it you think about it the same holds true for gold and silver which have a value mostly because someone is willing to pay that much for them.

I once had a ranch worker who thought she had thousands of dollars worth of Suffolk sheep because she had paid hundreds of dollars for her founding pair. She didn't believe me when I explained that nothing has value unless someone is willing to pay so much for it.

In fact she was insulted and kept insisting that her small flock was worth a lot of money, at least until she tried to sell them at auction and found everyone else saw them as mutton worth only $40 or $50 each.

People don't understand money or value and may become extremely upset when you try to explain economics to them.

As with sheep or stray cats, fiat currencies are only worth what someone else is willing to pay for them.

Digital mining (performing complex calculations on a computer) is what creates Bitcoins - you can make your own, but this indicates another way to value a Bitcoin - it is so difficult to calculate a new digital Bitcoin that it not only requires a bank of expensive computers or a supercomputer, and a significant amount of electricity.

Mining is essentially the process of generating a verifiable bookkeeping trail of a single coin.

The coins themselves are "owned" by individuals who hold a secret key to the wallet containing their coins. These keys are long and usually stored on a computer. One individual discarded the old hard drive holding his key and, since the key itself is the only way to prove ownership, that hard drive was worth about $7.5 MILLION. It is estimated that about $20 billion worth of Bitcoins have been lost forever, and about $7 billion have been stolen.

NOTE - it is useful to remember that the Bitcoin was invented around 2007-08 when the world economy was facing collapse and banks were being bailed out by governments because of the banks' terrible investment practices and the government's (George Bush) poor financial policies and complete deregulation of the banks leaving them to essentially invent new money backed by absolutely nothing.

Their new financial instruments looked as if they had value until, as with Dutch tulip bulbs, one day they tried to sell them and no one was willing to buy.

Unfortunately, Bitcoins turned out to be no more stable than any other fiat currency with the value of a single Bitcoin varying between about $.30 US to nearly $20,000 (actually thought to be about $19,666.)

The theft and loss of billions of dollars worth of Bitcoins point out another weakness of any fiat currency.

Governments (such as the U.S.) facing gigantic debts (about $20 trillion at the end of 2018 for the U.S.)

have an easy way out with fiat currency. They can reduce their national debt overnight without raising taxes or reducing spending by simply devaluing their money. In the case of the U.S., this could mean that one day a $100 bill would be worth $100 in goods and services and the next perhaps only $50.

The upside of that official devaluation is that the debt is now only half as difficult to pay off.

Unfortunately there is a considerable downside for people holding those dollars in their bank accounts.

If they own real estate or stocks, or gold, then the value of those holdings will almost instantly double as a consequence of the currency only being worth half as much. However, if people actually have their wealth held as an actual fiat currency, they are immediately worth only half as much.

Of course, that could never happen.

But, on the other hand, yes it could and has happened. President Nixon did it last officially (as opposed to merely letting inflation happen) in the U.S. during 1971 when the U.S. dollar was finally taken off the gold standard, completing the move begun by FDR in 1933 when he made it illegal for Americans to own gold bullion.

(Please look this up - I know from experience that well educated and wealthy businessmen didn't believe me when I said that it might become illegal to own gold or that the dollar could, and almost certainly will be devalued again. They thought it could never happen and flatly said they didn't believe me when I pointed out that it had been illegal in the U.S. for any individual to own, hold, possess, or store gold bullion from 1933 until mid-1971 subject to confiscation, fines, and possible imprisonment.)

After 1971 it became legal to own gold and the metal instantly surged in value - the other way of saying that is that the U.S. dollar went down in value - that is, it was devalued.

It could happen tomorrow, which is why most rich people have very little cash in banks.

Devaluing their currency isn't limited to the U.S.; most governments do it either formally or informally (by printing more paper money a.k.a. reducing the reserves required of banks also known as monetary easing).

The Pound Sterling was officially devalued 14% in 1969 and famously in 1976 when the Pound first dropped to less than $2 in value and financier George Soros bet against the Pound and made about $1 billion overnight.

The U.S. dollar is about 200 years old, the British Pound about 1,000 years old and both get both informal and formal devaluations as felt necessary by the governments of the time.

So you now know about all most people need to understand about Bitcoins and other cryptocurrencies - they are fiat currencies, just like paper money. The big difference is that governments declare the value of paper money while no central authority determines the value if any, of a cryptocurrency.

Chapter 11 Mining - Creating Your Own Money

Because you hear about it everyplace AND because it was the driving force behind the development of blockchain, Bitcoins are fascinating to many and while it would be an incredibly expensive and difficult for you to create a new Bitcoin for yourself, there are other cryptocurrencies and you could create your own.

Therefore I am going to explain in some detail just how to create your own Bitcoins that have actual value.

I want to make it clear at the outset that this would be a very bad idea - you don't want to do this, but it is important to see how it works.

About 17 million individual Bitcoins have been created, some lost, some stolen, but that many were created.

It is possible to create about four million new Bitcoins and I will explain just how to do this, but it is VERY expensive - each new group of Bitcoins is harder to create than the previous one.

The rate at which new Bitcoins can be created was defined by the creator in a paper published in 2008, "Bitcoin: A Peer-to-Peer Electronic Cash System" https://bitcoin.org/bitcoin.pdf by Satoshi Nakamoto.

Abstract.

"A purely peer-to-peer version of electronic cash would allow online payments to be sent directly from one party to another without going through a financial institution. Digital signatures provide part of the solution, but the main benefits are lost if a trusted third party is still required to prevent double-spending. We propose a solution to the double-spending problem using a peer-to-peer network. The network timestamps transactions by hashing them into an ongoing chain of hash-based proof-of-work, forming a record that cannot be changed without redoing the proof-of-work. The longest chain not only serves as proof of the sequence of events witnessed, but proof that it came from the largest pool of CPU power. As long as a majority of CPU power is controlled by nodes that are not cooperating to attack the network, they'll generate the longest chain and outpace attackers. The network itself requires minimal structure. Messages are broadcast on a best effort basis, and nodes can leave and rejoin the network at will, accepting the longest proof-of-work chain as proof of what happened while they were gone."

This is a relatively brief document considering how much commotion and value has been tied to it.

The paper goes into more detail than I do here, but since it includes terms such as "Binomial Random Walk," it is not as accessible.

Also, you won't find the word "blockchain" anywhere in the paper so it really isn't useful for most readers and, except for this chapter, my booklet is aimed at practical information for business users.

To mine Bitcoins you add records to the public ledger of the Bitcoin network.
These records go into a new block and new blocks are created several times each hour.

To become a Bitcoin miner you need special software such as the GUIMiner found at https://guiminer.org/.

This software runs the calculations needed to

create a new record. This is very difficult so there is a reward, the block reward, consisting of several Bitcoins awarded for each new solution.

The reward began at 50 Bitcoins before 2010 but every 210,000 blocks, approximately every four years, the amount is cut in half, to 25 Bitcoins in 2014.

You could do this on a PC in the early days but is so difficult now that there is a special Integrated Circuit just to do the mining calculations. But newer, faster ASICs (Application-Specific Integrated Circuits) are constantly being created.

In addition, the processing power is so immense that it is actually very expensive in terms of electricity Megawatts to produce a new record.

Bitcoin records and blocks are encrypted using the cryptographic hash function, the above mentioned SHA-256, to be specific.

This tool can create a relatively unique string of characters of a fixed length, known as a "hash". Using the tool is called "hashing."

The hash is currently impossible to guess in advance - miners keep trying different inputs until they generate a specific hash value.

The level of difficulty is changed about every two weeks.

As of 2018 it takes on average many trillions of these tries before someone finds the correct hash value - that person gets 12.5 Bitcoins as payment.

If for some reason this actually seems like something you would like to try, be aware that there is a massive amount of very experienced competition and, while you may be able to pay for the great deal of hardware necessary to compete, you may not be able to pay the electric bill to run that equipment.

Also be prepared to add massive cooling equipment such as a dedicated air conditioner and several fans because if you have any chance of success your computer will run at 100 percent capacity for long periods.

As an example, I have a quad processor with loads of memory, am running two browsers with 13 tabs open, and no actual work except running this cloud word processor, and my CPU load is currently 27 percent.

During mining it would be 100 percent on all four processors and my current setup would quickly overheat.

Appendix I Resources

For the very latest research on blockchain perform this search: https://scholar.google.com/scholar?hl=en&as_sdt=0,39&q=blockchain&scisbd=1

Older articles and papers

"A complete beginner's guide to blockchain," Bernard Marr, *Forbes*, January 24, 2017, https://www.forbes.com/sites/bernardmarr/2017/01/24/a-complete-beginners-guide-to-blockchain/#232ccc326e60.

"What is a blockchain, and why is it growing in popularity?" Alistair Dabbs, *ArsTechnica*, November 6, 2016, https://arstechnica.com/information-technology/2016/11/what-is-blockchain/.

"Blockchains: Moving digital government forward in the states," National Association of State Chief Information Officers (NASCIO), published May 2017, https://www.nascio.org/Publications/ArtMID/485/ArticleID/496/Blockchains-Moving-Digital-Government-Forward-in-the-States.

"If blockchains ran the world – Disrupting the trust business," *Economist*, July 6, 2017, http://worldif.economist.com/article/13525/disrupting-trust-business.

"A brief history of blockchain," Vinay Gupta, *Harvard Business Review*, February 28, 2017, available from https://hbr.org/2017/02/a-brief-history-of-blockchain.

"IBM goes live with first commercial blockchains," Michael del Castillo, *Coindesk*, March 20, 2017, https://www.coindesk.com/ibm-goes-live-first-commercial-blockchains/.

"The blockchain might be the next disruptive technology," Florian Graillot, *TechCrunch*, October 3, 2015 https://techcrunch.com/2015/10/03/the-blockchain-might-be-the-next-disruptive-technology/.

"Using the blockchain to fight crime and save lives," Andrew Thomson, *TechCrunch*, September 27, 2015, https://techcrunch.com/2015/09/27/using-the-blockchain-to-the-fight-crime-and-save-lives/.

-30-

www.ingramcontent.com/pod-product-compliance
Lightning Source LLC
Chambersburg PA
CBHW031549210526
45464CB00003B/1229